THE RISE OF
WESTERN SOCIETY

SAILING SHIPS AND REVOLUTIONS

Thanks to the creative team:
Senior Editor: Alice Peebles
Consultant: John Haywood
Fact Checking: Tom Jackson
Designer: Lauren Woods and collaborate agency

Hungry Tomato®
A division of Lerner Publishing Group, Inc.
241 First Avenue North
Minneapolis, MN 55401 USA

For reading levels and more information, look up
this title at www.lernerbooks.com.

Main body text set in Avenir Next Medium 10/12
Typeface provided by Linotype AG.

Library of Congress Cataloging-in-Publication Data

The Cataloging-in-Publication Data for *The Rise of Western Society:
Sailing Ships and Revolutions* is on file at the Library of Congress.
ISBN 978-1-5124-5973-9 (lib. bdg.)
ISBN 978-1-5124-9875-2 (eb pdf)

Manufactured in the United States of America
1-43032-27701-10/12/2017

THE RISE OF
WESTERN SOCIETY
SAILING SHIPS AND REVOLUTIONS

by John Farndon
Illustrated by Christian Cornia

HUNGRY
TOMATO®

Minneapolis

CONTENTS

In the book, some dates have c. before them.
This is short for "circa," or "about," showing
that an exact date is not known.

North America

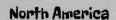

In the north, many Europeans came to settle as farmers. They saw it as empty land, though it was already home to many native peoples. In 1776, British settlers broke away from Britain to found their own independent country, the United States of America.

South America

As Europeans arrived in the Americas, native peoples were pushed aside, turned into slaves, or simply killed. European diseases also ravaged local populations. Spain and Portugal soon had South and Central America firmly under their thumbs.

SAILING SHIPS AND REVOLUTIONS

Between 1500 and 1900, Europe was where it was all happening. The rest of the world might have wanted a quiet life, but those noisy Europeans kept sending out ships to every corner of the globe to conquer, colonize, and trade. First, the Portuguese and Spanish did this, then the English, Dutch, French, and Germans. They changed the world forever.

Asia

After sending boats to explore the world in the 15th century, the Ming emperors of China kept to themselves. The Japanese, after centuries of warring, also settled down to a long period of calm in the Edo period. But even here, Europeans eventually made their presence felt.

Europe

Europeans fought war after war. But the continent buzzed with ideas and changes. Some were peaceful, like discoveries in science and the Industrial Revolution that brought the first factories. Less peaceful were the Reformation that split the Christian church, civil war in England, and the French Revolution.

Eurasia

Eurasia was dominated by the empire of the Ottoman Turks with its luxurious capital at Constantinople. The Ottomans repeatedly invaded Europe—and were repeatedly rebuffed by Christian European armies.

Africa

Europeans dragged Africans to the Americas to be slaves, then began to take Africa over in the 1800s. Each European country claimed a share, ignoring the locals. Much of Africa remained unknown to Europeans, though, until explorers began to trek deep into its heart.

Map Key
★ On the maps, major battles are shown by this symbol.

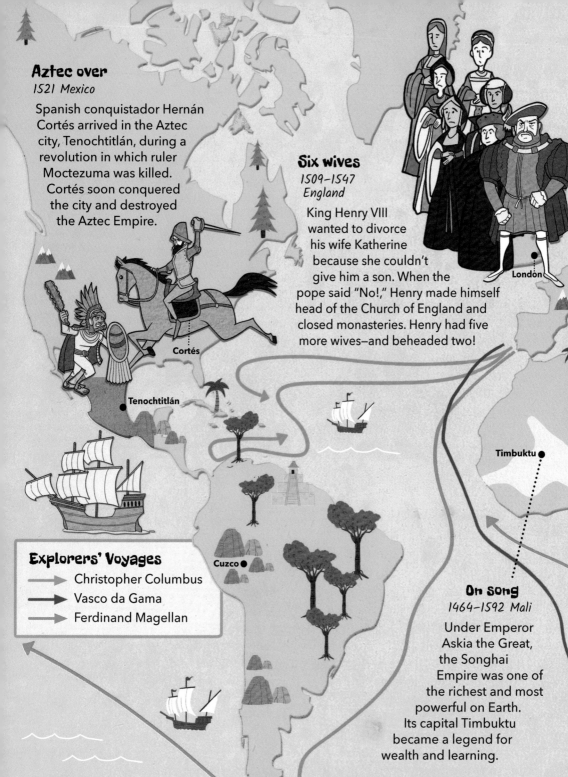

Aztec over
1521 Mexico

Spanish conquistador Hernán Cortés arrived in the Aztec city, Tenochtitlán, during a revolution in which ruler Moctezuma was killed. Cortés soon conquered the city and destroyed the Aztec Empire.

Cortés

Tenochtitlán

Six wives
1509–1547 England

King Henry VIII wanted to divorce his wife Katherine because she couldn't give him a son. When the pope said "No!," Henry made himself head of the Church of England and closed monasteries. Henry had five more wives—and beheaded two!

London

Timbuktu

Explorers' Voyages
→ Christopher Columbus
→ Vasco da Gama
→ Ferdinand Magellan

Cuzco

On song
1464–1592 Mali

Under Emperor Askia the Great, the Songhai Empire was one of the richest and most powerful on Earth. Its capital Timbuktu became a legend for wealth and learning.

1500	1502	1503	1517	1520	1521
Ottomans win sea battle at Lepanto	First African slaves in Americas	Leonardo paints the *Mona Lisa*	Luther makes his *95 Theses* public	Suleiman I rules Ottoman Empire	Cortés conquers the Aztecs

Copper knickers
1543 Poland

People once thought the sun and stars went around Earth. Polish astronomer Copernicus suggested Earth travels around the sun. Then Galileo proved it in 1610 with a new invention, the telescope.

Sultan Suleiman
1520–1566 Turkey

Suleiman I made the Ottoman Empire very powerful. Turkish people call him "the Lawgiver" because of his wise laws. Europeans called him "the Magnificent" because of his luxury lifestyle.

POLAND

Constantinople

I want to live forever!
1521–1567 China

Ming emperor Jiajing tortured or killed anyone who disagreed with him. But the empire started to crumble. He hired alchemists to make him live forever. Luckily, he didn't.

●Nanjing

Magellan's ship

CATHOLICS VS. PROTESTANTS
1500–1550

The Reformation ripped Europe apart and set countries at war. Catholic Christians believed the pope in Rome was boss. But in the north, Protestants, inspired by German priest Martin Luther, protested that they could pray to God without the pope—or fancy Latin words!

Round the world
1519–1522

Ship after ship sailed from Europe to explore the world and get spices from Indonesia. In 1519-1522, Portuguese captain Magellan's ship *Victoria* sailed around the world, though he was killed midway.

1521	1522	1532	1536	1543	1547
Jiajing becomes Chinese emperor	Magellan's ship sails round the world	King Henry VIII breaks from Rome	Queen Anne Boleyn beheaded	Copernicus asserts Earth orbits the sun	Ivan the Terrible first tsar of Russia

SPANISH GOLD
1550–1600

This was Spain's Golden Age. Big ships called galleons sailed back from the Americas stuffed with gold, helping to make Spain mega-rich and powerful under King Philip II. Painters such as El Greco and writers such as Cervantes made it a Golden Age for Spanish arts too.

Armada than you
1588 English Channel

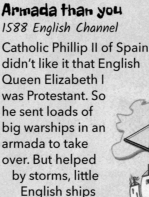

Catholic Phillip II of Spain didn't like it that English Queen Elizabeth I was Protestant. So he sent loads of big warships in an armada to take over. But helped by storms, little English ships beat them off.

Paris ●

Lost colony
1585 North America

In 1585, the English set up a colony on Roanoke Island (North Carolina). But when ships came from England in 1590, they found only an abandoned fort.

● Roanoke

Madrid

Algiers

Inca over
1533 Peru

Twelve years after Cortés conquered the Aztecs, the great Inca Empire fell to Spanish conquistador Francisco Pizarro. Pizarro had Inca emperor Atahualpa killed and made the Incas slaves.

Pizarro

Cuzco

Map Key

- Spanish Empire
- Russian Empire
- Ming dynasty
- Ottoman Empire
- Mughal Empire

1556	1556	1556	1572	1585
Akbar the Great is Mughal emperor	Worst earthquake ever in China	Philip II begins Spain's Golden Age	St. Bartholomew's Day Massacre of Protestants in France	Hideyoshi rules Japan as regent

Awesome Ivan
1547–1584 Russia

The Russian tsar (ruler) Ivan IV was called Ivan the Terrible because he often got really angry—so angry that he killed his own son. He made Russia much, much bigger by conquering Siberia in the east.

Muscovy

CHINA

Broken China
1556 Shaanxi, China

Poor people in China lived in *yaodongs* built into hills like caves. When an earthquake struck, yaodongs collapsed and 830,000 people died—the deadliest quake ever.

Barbary Coast

Tripoli

Corsairs
1530–1780 North Africa

For centuries, pirates from North Africa called corsairs raided ships and coastal villages in the western Mediterranean to capture slaves to sell to Ottoman princes. Corsairs also raided as far north as Iceland.

Agra

Akbar
1556–1605 India

Muslim emperor Akbar the Great made the Mughal Empire super-powerful in India—not just by his military victories but also by making friends and giving space for different religions in the empire.

1587	**1587**	**1588**	**c. 1593**	**1599**	**1600**
Mary, Queen of Scots, executed	Abbas becomes shah of Persia	English defeat Spanish Armada	Shakespeare writes *Romeo and Juliet*	Mali Empire defeated at Jenné	Japan begins Edo period

11

Roundheads vs. Cavaliers
1642–1651 England

Civil war broke out in England when Parliament got fed up with King Charles I. Parliament's army (Roundheads) beat the Royalists (Cavaliers), and Charles was beheaded. Roundhead Oliver Cromwell then ruled England for a while.

London

Plymouth

Pilgrim Fathers
1620 Plymouth, Massachusetts, N. America

In 1620, the *Mayflower* sailed from Plymouth, England, to North America, carrying 102 pilgrims fleeing persecution for their Puritan beliefs. Pilgrim William Bradford's diaries show how tough their new life was, but they survived, and more settlers soon followed.

THE WORLD TURNED UPSIDE DOWN
1600–1650

European merchants sailed out to places like India and brought back riches, which created a Golden Age for the Dutch. But back home there was chaos as people questioned the power of kings, bringing civil war to England and France and the Thirty Years' War in central Europe.

1603
Tokugawa Ieyasu starts Edo in Japan

1605
Gunpowder Plot in England

1606
Willem Janszoon reaches Australia

1607
Irish earls flee to Europe

1607
Jamestown, Virginia, founded

1608
Founding of Quebec

Swede power
1611–1632 Sweden

King Gustavus Adolphus made Sweden a great power with his military genius in the Thirty Years' War. But he got lost in the fog and was killed at the Battle of Lützen.

Super Louis
1643–1715 France

French king Louis XIV was such a star he was known as the Sun King. He built the mega-glamorous palace of Versailles for himself.

Leiden
Delft
Versailles
Paris

Russian rule
1613–1917 Russia

Russia was in a mess, so in 1613 Russian boyars (lords) made 16-year-old Mikhail Romanov the tsar. Amazingly, it worked, and the Romanovs were tsars for 300 years.

● Moscow

Dutch Golden Age
1600s Netherlands

Holland may have been small, but in the 1600s its ships traded the world over, making it rich. Dutch towns, such as Leiden and Delft, buzzed with brilliant scientists like Christiaan Huygens and artists like Jan Vermeer.

Pisa

Tunis

Samurai power
1603–1868 Japan

Warlords fought over Japan with armies of samurai warriors. In 1603, warlord Tokugawa Ieyasu came out on top, starting a time of peace named after the capital city of Edo (now called Tokyo).

● Edo

Science genius
1564–1642 Italy

Galileo made brilliant experiments on how things move, proved Earth orbits the sun and discovered that Jupiter has moons. But his ideas upset the pope, and he was arrested.

1613	**1618**	**1620**	**1632**	**1642**	**1644**
House of Romanov begins in Russia	Thirty Years' War starts, central Europe	Czechs defeated at White Mountain	Taj Mahal begun in India	English Civil War begins	The Qing end Ming dynasty in China

Bewitched
1692 North America

People were really worried about witchcraft. When girls from Salem, Massachusetts, accused some women (and a few men) of being witches, 20 people were tried and hanged.

Niagara

Salem

Mississippi
Louisiana

What goes up
1687 England

An apple falling from a tree inspired Isaac Newton's theory of gravity. He also devised three key laws of motion.

London

Prague

Paris   **Vienna**

Going Orange *1688 England*

The English Parliament brought in Protestant William of Orange as king to replace Catholic James II. William beat James at the Boyne in Ireland.

WARS AND WITCHES
1650–1700

There were lots of wars in Europe at this time, with the French fighting the Holy Roman Empire and the Holy Roman Empire fighting the Ottoman Turks, for starters. But in North America, the new European colonies seemed more bothered by witches . . .

Gold rush *1693*

In 1693, news got out that gold had been found in Minas Gerais in southern Brazil. At once, lots of people rushed there hoping to strike it lucky. It was the real beginning of Brazil.

Minas Gerais

São Paulo

1652	1660	1664	1666	1670	1673
Cape Town founded, S. Africa	England gets a king again, Charles II	New Amsterdam becomes New York	London burned down in Great Fire	Hudson Bay Company founded	Van Leeuwenhoek discovers bacteria

Sulky sultan
1683 Constantinople

The Ottoman Turks were always trying to conquer Christian Europe. In 1683, Grand Vizier (big boss) Kara Mustafa got to Vienna but was defeated by the Polish king, John Sobieski. The sultan had Kara killed as a result.

Close shave 1661 China

Emperor Kangxi wanted the Chinese to know for sure that it was the Qing family in charge now, not the Ming. So he told all men to shave their heads "queue-style" but wear very long pigtails!

• Constantinople

In memory
1653 India

The Mughal (Indian Muslim) emperor Shah Jahan built his wife, Mumtaz Mahal, the world's most beautiful burial place, the Taj Mahal at Agra.

Map Key
- Polish-Lithuanian Empire
- Ming dynasty
- Ottoman Empire
- Mughal Empire

1674	1682	1683	1688	1688	1690
Marathas begin to replace Mughals in India	Peter the Great is tsar in Russia	Ottomans defeated at Vienna	William of Orange is king of England	France and Holy Roman Empire at war	Battle of the Boyne in Northern Ireland

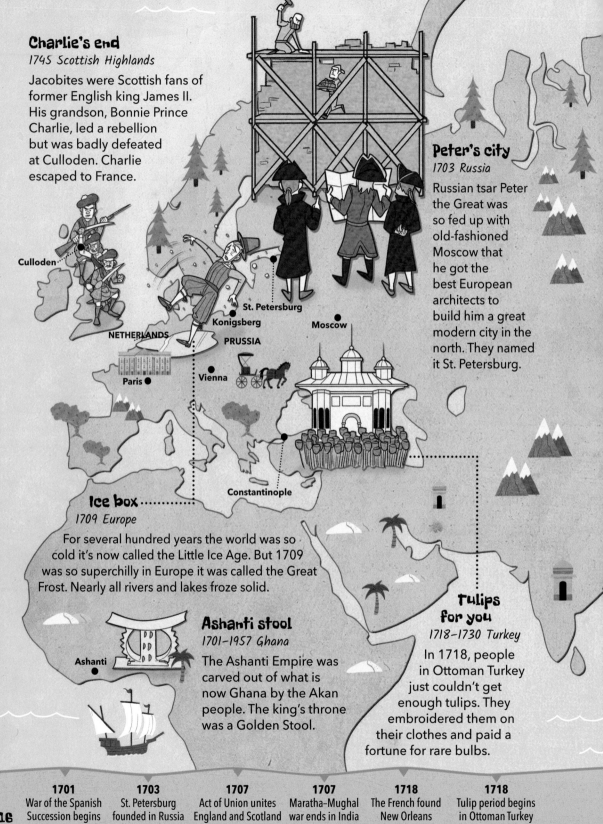

Charlie's end
1745 Scottish Highlands

Jacobites were Scottish fans of former English king James II. His grandson, Bonnie Prince Charlie, led a rebellion but was badly defeated at Culloden. Charlie escaped to France.

Culloden

Peter's city
1703 Russia

Russian tsar Peter the Great was so fed up with old-fashioned Moscow that he got the best European architects to build him a great modern city in the north. They named it St. Petersburg.

St. Petersburg
Konigsberg
Moscow
NETHERLANDS
PRUSSIA
Paris
Vienna
Constantinople

Ice box
1709 Europe

For several hundred years the world was so cold it's now called the Little Ice Age. But 1709 was so superchilly in Europe it was called the Great Frost. Nearly all rivers and lakes froze solid.

Ashanti stool
1701–1957 Ghana

The Ashanti Empire was carved out of what is now Ghana by the Akan people. The king's throne was a Golden Stool.

Ashanti

Tulips for you
1718–1730 Turkey

In 1718, people in Ottoman Turkey just couldn't get enough tulips. They embroidered them on their clothes and paid a fortune for rare bulbs.

1701	**1703**	**1707**	**1707**	**1718**	**1718**
War of the Spanish Succession begins	St. Petersburg founded in Russia	Act of Union unites England and Scotland	Maratha-Mughal war ends in India	The French found New Orleans	Tulip period begins in Ottoman Turkey

Yeongjo
1724–1776 Korea

King Yeongjo was a wise king who promoted fairness and awarded merit, following the Chinese ideas of Confucius. But his son Sado was a cruel man who killed and hurt many people. So Yeongjo had him trapped in a rice chest until he died.

KOREA ●

Shiver me timbers!
1716–1726 Caribbean

Pirate ships roamed the Caribbean, attacking Spanish ships carrying gold and other riches. Ruthless pirates like Blackbeard and Anne Bonny became famous.

THE AGE OF REASON
1700–1750

There was plenty of trouble around the world, but historians call this the Age of Reason. That's because a new breed of thinkers showed that science and logic—not superstition—were the way forward and that every man and woman has natural rights.

1721	1723	1735	1740	1744	1745
Horace Walpole first British prime minister	Kazakhs suffer Dzunghar invasion	Yeghevard: Persians defeat Ottomans	Frederick the Great is king of Prussia	Mohammed Ibn Saud founds Saudi state	Second Jacobite rising in Scotland

CANADA

War around the world
1756–1763

Rivalry between France and Britain started a global war, the Seven Years' War. In the end, the French handed chilly North America, including Canada, to the British and took two warm, sugar-rich Caribbean islands instead.

The American way
1787 USA

In 1776, Britain's 13 colonies in North America declared they were no longer part of Britain but the United States. After a war, Britain agreed. Four years later, Americans wrote their own remarkable rules for governing themselves: the US Constitution.

Philadelphia ●

Haiti's Napoleon
1791–1804 Haiti

When the French revolutionaries broke their promise to free slaves, black slaves on the French island of Haiti fought back. The brilliant leadership of former slave Toussaint L'Ouverture won the day for the slaves, and Haiti became independent in 1804.

HAITI

Map Key
Conflict areas of the Seven Years' War

1755	1756	1757	1762	1771	1773
Earthquake destroys Lisbon	Seven Years' War begins	Battle of Plassey starts British rule in India	Catherine II is empress of Russia	Arkwright builds first powered factory	Pugachev's peasant revolt in Russia

Factory power
1760–1830 Britain

The Industrial Revolution started in Britain. Things were made on a huge scale in factories, using machines powered by water, then steam. Soon industrial cities filled the landscape.

Cromford (first powered factory)

Catherine the Great
1762–1798 Russia

When her husband, Tsar Peter III, was assassinated, Catherine II became empress of Russia. She was perhaps Russia's greatest ruler, making it a major power and cultivating the arts.

St. Petersburg

People power *1789–1799 France*

In 1789, the French rebelled and declared France a republic. Crowds cheered as king and lords were beheaded by the guillotine. The French Revolution changed the world but was chaotic and bloody.

Britain in India
1757 India

After a crucial victory at Plassey for the British under Robert Clive, India fell under British control for 200 years.

Plassey

REVOLUTION AND INDEPENDENCE
1750–1800

Ideas about natural rights made people realize just how much they were put upon by kings and lords. The French rose in revolution against their king and lords. Americans fought a war against the British and declared themselves independent.

1776	**1787**	**1789**	**1789**	**1791**	**1794**
American Declaration of Independence	United States Constitution written	French Revolution begins	George Washington is first US president	Haitian revolution	White Lotus Revolution in China

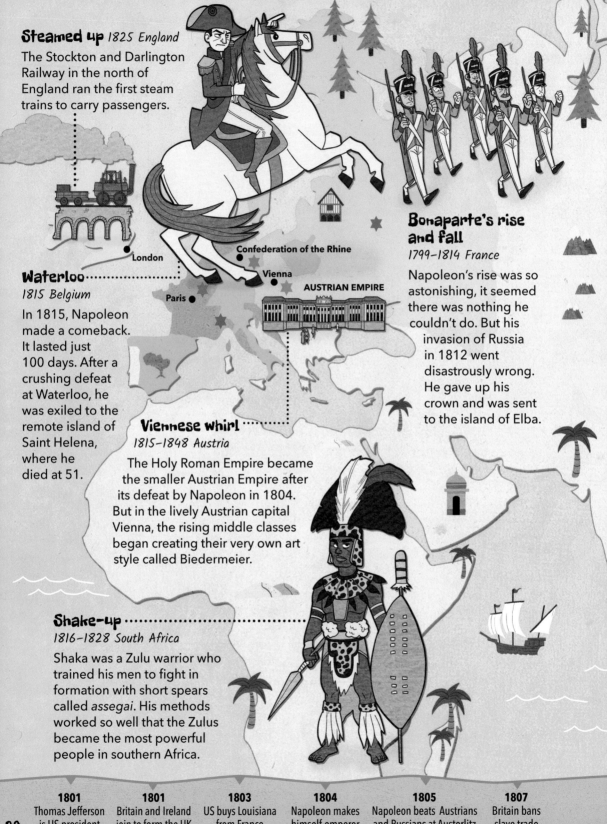

Steamed up *1825 England*

The Stockton and Darlington Railway in the north of England ran the first steam trains to carry passengers.

Waterloo

1815 Belgium

In 1815, Napoleon made a comeback. It lasted just 100 days. After a crushing defeat at Waterloo, he was exiled to the remote island of Saint Helena, where he died at 51.

London

Confederation of the Rhine

Vienna

Paris

AUSTRIAN EMPIRE

Bonaparte's rise and fall

1799–1814 France

Napoleon's rise was so astonishing, it seemed there was nothing he couldn't do. But his invasion of Russia in 1812 went disastrously wrong. He gave up his crown and was sent to the island of Elba.

Viennese whirl

1815–1848 Austria

The Holy Roman Empire became the smaller Austrian Empire after its defeat by Napoleon in 1804. But in the lively Austrian capital Vienna, the rising middle classes began creating their very own art style called Biedermeier.

Shake-up

1816–1828 South Africa

Shaka was a Zulu warrior who trained his men to fight in formation with short spears called *assegai*. His methods worked so well that the Zulus became the most powerful people in southern Africa.

| **1801**
Thomas Jefferson is US president | **1801**
Britain and Ireland join to form the UK | **1803**
US buys Louisiana from France | **1804**
Napoleon makes himself emperor | **1805**
Napoleon beats Austrians and Russians at Austerlitz | **1807**
Britain bans slave trade |

NAPOLEON ON THE MARCH

1800–1825 Europe

In the chaos of the French Revolution, young Napoleon Bonaparte took over as head of the army. A brilliant general, Napoleon led the army to victory after victory across Europe, creating a large French Empire and making himself emperor in 1804.

Napoleon's Europe in 1810

- French Empire
- Dependent states
- At war with Napoleon
- Napoleon's allies

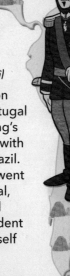

Brazil arrives

1822–1831 Brazil

When Napoleon conquered Portugal in 1807, the king's son Pedro fled with his family to Brazil. When his dad went back to Portugal, Pedro declared Brazil independent and made himself emperor.

Major Battles

- ★ Marengo 1800
- ★ Austerlitz 1805
- ★ Moscow 1812
- ★ Leipzig 1813
- ★ Waterloo 1815

1815	**1816**	**1820**	**1821**	**1821**	**1822**
Congress of Vienna ends Napoleonic Wars	Shaka leads the Zulus	Maratha Empire ends in India	Greece independent from the Ottomans	Mexico and Peru independent from Spain	Brazil independent from Portugal

Hot wires
1844 USA

The invention of the electric telegraph meant that, for the first time, messages could be sent instantly over long distances simply by switching the power on and off in the code pattern invented by Samuel Morse.

Irish tragedy
1845–1848 Ireland

Poor Irish country people relied entirely on potatoes for food. So when a disease called blight ruined the potato crop, a million Irish starved to death and a million more were forced to emigrate.

London

IRELAND

Washington, DC

Oklahoma

Georgia

Trail of Tears
1838 USA

Many Native Americans were driven from their land. In 1838, Cherokees were forced to leave their home in Georgia to trek to Oklahoma. On the way 4,000 died, which is why it is called the Trail of Tears.

Slaves no more
1833 British Empire

After years of campaigning by William Wilberforce, the British government realized at last that slavery was so wrong it should be against the law. From 1833, all slaves in the British Empire were set free.

CHANGING WORLD
1825–1850

The Industrial Revolution was spreading, and huge new cities appeared. Many people in Europe were still fired up by the ideas of the French Revolution and demanded political change too. But there was still much suffering among the world's poor and dispossessed.

1825	1830	1833	1833	1834	1834
Black War against aboriginal Tasmanians	Belgium created	Slavery abolished in British Empire	Carlist wars begin in Spain	German Customs Union formed	Texan separatists defeated at the Alamo

A poet's death
1837 Russia

St. Petersburg

Russia's greatest poet Alexander Pushkin often upset the authorities with his outspoken views. But he was killed in a duel, aged just 37, by an army officer who flirted with Pushkin's beautiful wife, Natalia.

Listen to us!
1848 Europe

Poor people in Europe were fed up with having no say in their lives. So in 1848 they started revolutions in over 50 countries, including France and Austria. All serfs (peasants) in Austria were then given their freedom.

● German Customs Union

Paris

Vienna

China wars
1839–1842 and 1856–1860 China

Hong Kong

China tried to stop the British selling the drug opium there, so the British twice went to war. They won the freedom to trade in China and the port of Hong Kong.

Get the picture
1825 France

Frenchman Nicéphore Niépce created the world's first (very fuzzy!) photo. He used light-sensitive chemicals to record the image projected by a lens into a dark box called a camera.

Aboriginal tragedy
1825–1832 Australia

In the Black War, aboriginals in Tasmania fought to protect their hunting grounds from incoming Europeans. But in the end, all of them were killed.

Tasmania

1837	1837	1839	1845	1848	1848
Victoria is queen of the United Kingdom	Electric telegraph invented	First Opium War in China begins	Irish potato famine begins	Revolutions across Europe	California Gold Rush

NEW NATIONS
1850–1875

While the United States was split by a terrible civil war over the abolition of slavery, the British Empire grew to be the largest empire ever. Meanwhile, groups of small states in Europe that spoke the same language joined up to form the new nations of Germany and Italy.

Lincoln killed *1865 USA*

Abraham Lincoln was the great US president who championed the abolition of slavery and led the Union side to victory in the American Civil War. But just a few days after the war ended, Lincoln was shot dead in a theater in Washington.

Coast to coast *1869 USA*

In 1869 at Promontary, Utah, Southern Pacific Railroad president Leland Stanford drove in a golden spike (nail) to complete the transcontinental railway: the railway that ran right across the United States.

• Promontary, Utah

★ Gettysburg

★ Appomattox

Americans vs. Americans
1861–1865 USA

Southern states in the United States were upset when Lincoln pledged to abolish slavery in 1861. So they created the Confederate army and went to war against the Unionists in the North. After four terrible years, the Unionists won.

Map Key
- Union State or Territory
- Confederate States

1851	1853	1854	1857	1859	1861
Victoria gold rush in Australia	Crimean War begins	Japan ends its isolation	Indian rebellion against the British	Darwin publishes his theory of evolution	American Civil War begins

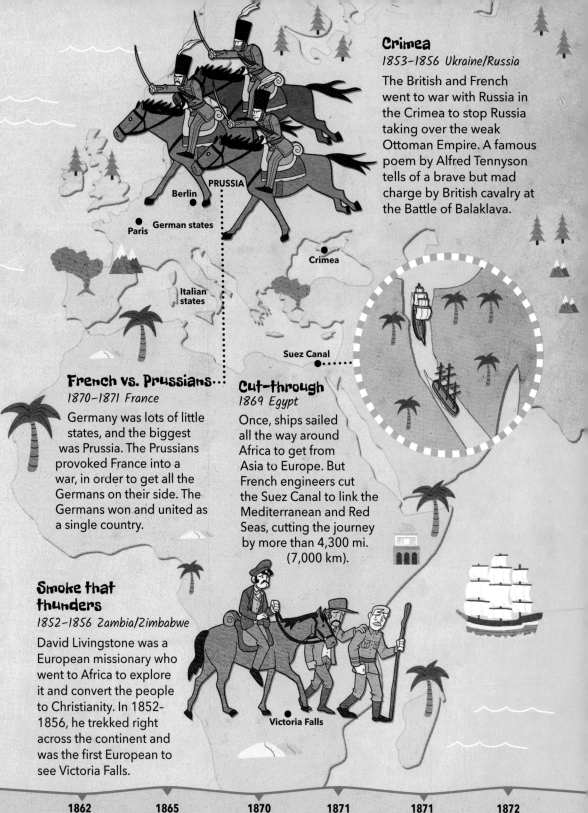

Crimea
1853–1856 Ukraine/Russia

The British and French went to war with Russia in the Crimea to stop Russia taking over the weak Ottoman Empire. A famous poem by Alfred Tennyson tells of a brave but mad charge by British cavalry at the Battle of Balaklava.

PRUSSIA

Berlin

German states

Paris

Crimea

Italian states

Suez Canal

French vs. Prussians...
1870–1871 France

Germany was lots of little states, and the biggest was Prussia. The Prussians provoked France into a war, in order to get all the Germans on their side. The Germans won and united as a single country.

Cut-through
1869 Egypt

Once, ships sailed all the way around Africa to get from Asia to Europe. But French engineers cut the Suez Canal to link the Mediterranean and Red Seas, cutting the journey by more than 4,300 mi. (7,000 km).

Smoke that thunders
1852–1856 Zambia/Zimbabwe

David Livingstone was a European missionary who went to Africa to explore it and convert the people to Christianity. In 1852–1856, he trekked right across the continent and was the first European to see Victoria Falls.

Victoria Falls

1862
Bismarck comes to power in Germany

1865
US president Lincoln assassinated

1870
Germany and Italy unified

1871
Paris Commune

1871
Stanley meets Livingstone in Africa

1872
First international football match

The first car
1885 Germany

German engineer Karl Benz built the first car, the Benz Patent Motorwagen, in 1885. Three years later, his wife, Bertha, took it out secretly for a 120-mi. (194-km) round-trip to see her mother. The car had arrived.

Boxer shorts
1899–1901 China

The Boxers were a Chinese group determined to punch foreigners out of China. They attacked Beijing and trapped foreign diplomats. But eight foreign nations got an army together to defeat the Boxers.

CHINA

Greek games
1896 Greece

In 1896 in Athens, sportsmen created a modern version of the Olympic Games of Ancient Greece. They have been held every four years since.

Moscow
Berlin
London
Paris
Athens

Big bang!
1883 Indonesia

The eruption of the volcanic island of Krakatoa was so loud, it would have deafened anyone within 9 mi. (15 km). It sent up so much ash that the world got over 33°F (1°C) cooler the next summer.

Tokyo

What a Boer!
1899–1902 South Africa

The Boer War was fought in southern Africa between the British and the Dutch settlers, known as Boers. The Boers were poor farmers but kept the British army at bay for years by guerrilla attacks.

Krakatoa

Scramble for Africa
1881–1914 Africa

SOUTH AFRICA

In 1870, only a tenth of Africa was in European control. But after talking in Berlin in 1881, European countries started a mad grab and had made nine-tenths of Africa theirs by 1914. The Africans had no say.

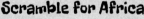

1876	1876	1876	1881	1881	1883
Bulgarians rebel against Ottomans	Famine kills 13 million in China	Battle of the Little Bighorn	Gunfight at the OK Corral, Arizona	Europeans begin taking over Africa	Krakatoa volcano erupts

Crazy Horse
c. 1842–1877 USA

Crazy Horse was a leader of the Oglala Lakota and a hero of Native American resistance to the European takeover of their lands. He helped lead them to their greatest victory at Little Bighorn in 1876.

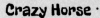

Little Bighorn

Mannheim

Lawmen vs. cowboys
1881 USA

Outlaws got away with murder in the American West. But at the famous gunfight at the OK Corral in Tombstone, Arizona, four lawmen led by Wyatt Earp, gunned down the infamous "Cowboys" in a 30-second shoot-out.

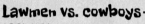

Tombstone

AMERICA MOVES ON WEST
1875–1900

In the United States, European settlers pushed on westwards, and Native Americans were driven from their lands. Meanwhile, European powers, such as Britain and Germany, were transformed by heavy industry and used their might to extend their control around the world.

1884	1890	1893	1896	1899	1899
Siege of British in Khartoum	Massacre of Native Americans, Wounded Knee	New Zealand allows women to vote	First modern Olympic Games	Boxer Rebellion in China	Boer War in southern Africa

WHO'S WHO

Many different groups of people played their part in the history of these times. Some had proper names like Incas and Mughals. But many were given names meant to insult them, such as Roundheads and Puritans.

Pope fans: Catholics
100 CE–present

Catholics are the biggest and oldest Christian church. They are headed by the pope in Rome, which is why they are called Roman Catholics. Catholics believe they can only reach God through priests.

100 CE

Chief people: Cherokee
1000–present

The Cherokee were Native American people who lived in the southeastern United States at least 1,000 years ago. The Europeans said they were one of the five "civilized" tribes in the early 1800s because they had adopted many European ideas.

Pluming marvels: Cavaliers
1642–1679

Cavaliers were the supporters of the king (Royalists) against Parliament in the English Civil War. They were famous for their big hats with feathers, their rich, colorful clothes, and their long, flowing hair.

High-powered Hindus: Marathas
1674–1818

The Maratha Empire was carved out in southern India by Hindu warriors from the Deccan Plateau. This empire came to dominate India as the Mughals' might weakened.

Crop tops: Roundheads
1642–1681

Roundheads were the supporters of Parliament (Parliamentarians) against the king in the English Civil War. The name came from opponents who mocked how their hair was cut short around their heads. They wore dull brown or yellow clothes.

Scots lot: Jacobites
1688–1746

Jacob is the Latin name for James. Jacobites were mainly those Scots who wanted to put the Catholic king, James II of England (James VII of Scotland), back on the English throne after he was deposed in 1688.

Dutch walkers: Boers
1750–present

The Boers were Dutch farmers who settled in southern Africa. The Voortrekkers were Boers who went on a Great Trek in 1835-1840 to find new lands away from the British.

Eastern power: Ottomans
1299–1923

The Ottomans came from northwest Anatolia in modern Turkey. When the Byzantine Empire collapsed in 1453, the Ottomans captured Constantinople and created their own huge empire.

Cuzco we can: Incas
1438–1533

The Incas built a huge empire from their capital city, Cuzco, high up in the Andean Mountains. They had no wheels or horses but built remarkable stone roads for walking.

Mex 'tecs: Aztecs
1427–1521

The Aztecs created a powerful empire from their lake city Tenochtitlán, where Mexico City is now. They were ruthless soldiers who made mass human sacrifices of their enemies to keep the gods happy.

Mighty Muslims: Mughals
1526–1857

The Mughals were the Muslim rulers of a huge empire that covered much of India for three centuries. The Mughal emperors claimed to have descended from the Mongol leader, Chinggis Khan.

No frills: Puritans *1558–1700*
Puritans were very serious English (later American) Protestants who wanted to stay utterly pure. They wanted to get rid of all the fancy trappings of the Catholic Church—and pretty much all fun, too.

French friends: Jacobins
1789–1794

The Jacobins were the French political club behind the French Revolution, and their year in government from 1793 was known as the Reign of Terror. Their most famous member was Maximilien de Robespierre.

Breakaway South: Confederates
1861–1865

Confederates were supporters of the southern US states that wanted to break away from the Union of the United States when President Lincoln promised to abolish slavery. They formed one side in the American Civil War.

United North: Unionists
1861–1865

Unionists were supporters of the US states (mostly from the northern states) who supported President Lincoln against the Confederates in the American Civil War.

1865

WELL, I NEVER...

Some strange stories from history.

CRAZY PIRATE

Blackbeard (1680-1718) was a fearsome pirate whose real name was Edward Teach. He was called Blackbeard because of his huge, black beard knotted into plaits that looked like writhing snakes. When he went into battle, he often tied lit fireworks into the plaits to make himself look superscary! In 1718, Blackbeard ran his ship the *Queen Anne's Revenge* aground in Beaufort Inlet, North Carolina, to evade capture. The wreck of the ship was found by divers in 1996.

DARING DRAKE

Francis Drake (1540-1596) was a daring English sea captain who was the first captain to sail around the world in one go. He didn't always play by the rules and often made illegal attacks on Spanish ships to capture treasure for Queen Elizabeth I. When news came that the Spanish Armada was attacking England, legend has it that he coolly finished the game of bowls (like bocce ball) he was playing on the Hoe (ridge) at Plymouth. His skillful captaincy played a key part in beating the Spanish.

KING OF THE WILD FRONTIER

Davy Crockett (1786–1836) was an American frontiersman who became a hero and was said to wear a hat made of raccoon skin. He was a great hunter, especially of bears, and there are many tales of his exploits. He famously saved President Jackson from a would-be killer. He became a member of Congress, but resigned in protest at Jackson's policy of removing the Native Americans from their lands. Later, he joined the Texas Separatists and was killed at the Battle of the Alamo.

BIG PETE

Peter the Great (1672–1725) was one of Russia's greatest tsars. He was really keen to learn about the latest developments in science and technology, so in 1698, he decided to travel to western Europe in disguise. He went to Holland and then worked in London as a humble shipwright, helping build ships. Mind you, few people were fooled. He was well over 6.5 ft. (2 m) tall and had a thick Russian accent.

INDEX

The Author

John Farndon is Royal Literary Fellow at City&Guilds in London, UK, and the author of a huge number of books for adults and children on science, technology and history, including international bestsellers. He has been shortlisted six times for the Royal Society's Young People's Book Prize, with titles such as *How the Earth Works* and *What Happens When?*

The Illustrator

Italian-born Christian Cornia decided at the age of four to be a comic-book artist, and is essentially self-taught. He works digitally, but always has a sketchbook in his bag. Cornia has illustrated Marvel Comics and is one of the artists for the Scooby-Doo character in Italy and the United States. He also teaches animation at the Scuola Internazionale di Comics in Italy.